Leatherback Turtle

Text and illustrations © 1992 Greey de
Pencier Books, 56 The Esplanade,
Suite 302, Toronto, Ontario, M5E 1A7.
All rights reserved.

ISBN 0-920775-90-X

OWL and the OWL colophon are
trademarks of the Young Naturalist
Foundation. Greey de Pencier Books is a
licensed user of these trademarks.

For permission to use copyrighted photos
we thank: Scott A. Eckert, pp.4/5, 14/15,
15, 16/17, 20/21, 26/27; Anne Heimann,
pp.11, 28/29, 29; Frans Lanting/Minden
Pictures, pp.8/9, 17, 31; Frans
Lanting/Photo Researchers Inc., p.21;
C.C. Lockwood/Bruce Coleman Inc.,
p.30.

We are grateful to Dr. Karen Eckert,
Executive Director, WIDECAST and Dr.
Nick Mrosovsky, University of Toronto,
for their assistance in the preparation of
this book.

Design by Word & Image Design Studio,
Toronto

Silhouette illustrations by Dave McKay

Research by Katherine Farris

Cover photo by Scott A. Eckert

Printed in Canada on recycled paper

A B C D E F

CANADA'S ENDANGERED ANIMALS

Leatherback Turtle

From OWL Magazine

Written by Sylvia Funston
Illustrated by Olena Kassian

Greey de Pencier Books

Introduction

Scientists describe certain animals as endangered to warn people that, unless we take special care, they will disappear forever from the world.

Many animals are endangered because people have taken over their wilderness homes. Others become endangered because they are over-hunted. Still others are endangered because pollution is poisoning them.

In this book you will discover how leatherback turtles live. You will explore the special reasons they are endangered and find out what is being done — as well as what you can do — to help them survive far into the future.

Turtle

QUIZ

Dive into the world of
leatherback turtles and see
how much you know about
these mysterious creatures.

Answers page 32

1. Leatherback turtles spend most of their
time:
a. swimming in the open sea
b. sunbathing on rocks
c. sleeping in caves.

2. Where does a female leatherback turtle lay
her eggs?
a. in an underwater cave
b. in a nest of seaweed
c. in a hole she digs on a beach

3. Leatherback turtles often die when they
get tangled in a fishing net because:
a. they cannot reach the surface to breathe
b. they are lonely
c. there is no food.

4. As soon as leatherback hatchlings reach the sea they:

a. hide among the seaweed

b. gather in large groups

c. swim as fast as possible for the open ocean.

5. When newly hatched leatherback turtles dash to the sea, what obstacles on the beach can slow them down?

a. little sea shells

b. tire marks

c. piles of seaweed

6. Leatherback turtle eggs are shaped like:

a. balls

b. chicken eggs

c. building blocks.

7. A leatherback turtle is a:

a. mammal

b. reptile

c. amphibian.

Going Home

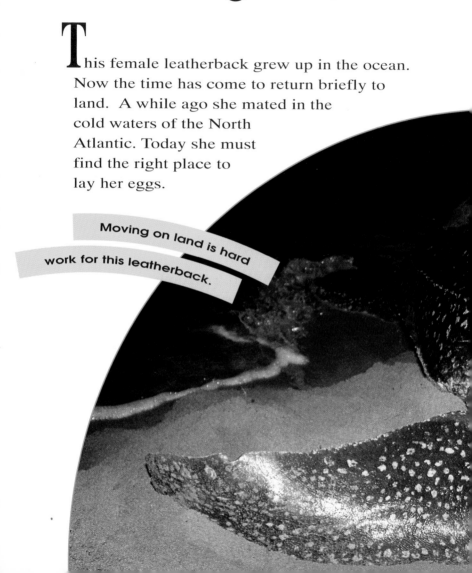

This female leatherback grew up in the ocean. Now the time has come to return briefly to land. A while ago she mated in the cold waters of the North Atlantic. Today she must find the right place to lay her eggs.

Moving on land is hard work for this leatherback.

Gliding gracefully through the warm Caribbean Sea, the turtle is heading for a special stretch of island coastline. It is the place where, one evening many years ago, she herself hatched from an egg.

The female turtle waits for night. Slowly, using all the strength in her powerful front flippers, she hauls her massive body out of the sea.

Out of the Sea

How can the female leatherback, after not being near land for many years, return without help to the coastline where she hatched?

Leatherbacks are such powerful swimmers, they seem to fly through the water.

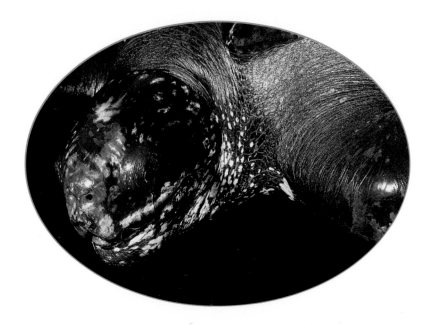

Scientists have discovered that sea turtles have a special substance in their foreheads that helps guide them like a compass. Perhaps leatherbacks use this to find their way in the sea. They might also be able to use ocean currents to tell them where they are. In addition, they might search for familiar smells in the water to tell them they are getting close to their home beach.

Working in the Dark

Once ashore, the female leatherback looks for a place above the high-water mark. Then she begins to dig steadily with her back flippers.

When the hole is as deep as her flippers are long, she lays more than a hundred eggs in it. Her eggs look like oversized, soft ping-pong balls and glisten white in the moonlight.

Quickly, the leatherback fills in her nest hole
with sand. She smooths the surface sand to hide
the location of her nest, then turns and drags
her huge body back to the sea.

Hundreds of Eggs

Over the summer months, the female leatherback hauls herself ashore several more times. Each time, she digs another nest and fills it with eggs before returning to the sea.

Leatherback eggs take two months to hatch.

Survival is difficult for young animals in the sea. By laying as many eggs as possible, the female leatherback increases the chances that one or two of her hatchlings will survive long enough to grow up.

Dangerous Crossing

Finally, hatching time arrives. One by one, little heads poke out of the sand and look around. The hatchlings see the dark shapes of trees in one direction, the clear, bright horizon of the sea in the other, and start running toward the sea.

Hatchlings wait until after dark before scrambling out of their nest.

The short journey the hatchlings must make across the open beach is full of danger. The lucky ones reach the safety of the waves. The rest are carried off by night herons or dogs, or are attacked by hungry crabs.

Survival in the Sea

The tiny leatherbacks that escape the predators of the beach soon learn that the sea is filled with other kinds of dangers.

Sharks and other large fish often cruise the waters off turtle beaches, waiting for the hatchlings to arrive.

Any leatherbacks that escape them swim as hard as they can straight out to the open sea.

What the young leatherbacks do then is a mystery. Perhaps one out of every 100 hatchlings manages to survive alone in the ocean. One day these survivors will mate and, if they are female, will make the incredible journey back to their home beach.

Leatherback Turtles Are Amazing

▶ Leatherbacks normally stay underwater for up to 15 minutes at a time. The longest recorded dive is 34 minutes.

▶ Female leatherbacks lay their eggs deep in the sand to keep the nest at a steady temperature. If the temperature rises above 29.5°C (85°F) the nest will produce mostly female hatchlings. If it drops, the hatchlings are more likely to be male.

- ► Leatherbacks go into colder water, dive deeper and travel farther than any other sea turtle. The longest recorded journey by a turtle — 5,900 km (3,660 miles) — was made by a leatherback.

- ► Every time a leatherback eats its favorite food — jellyfish — it swallows sea water. To get rid of harmful, excess salt from its body, the turtle cries nonstop.

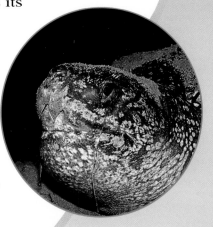

- ► The record number of nests dug by one female leatherback over a summer is 11. Most dig an average of six nests.

Some leatherbacks can weigh as much as a small car.

The Leatherback
Up Close

▶ The leatherback
is the only sea
turtle that has
no claws on
its flippers.

▶ Lining the
leatherback's mouth
and throat are
backward-facing
spines. They keep
slippery jellyfish
from escaping.

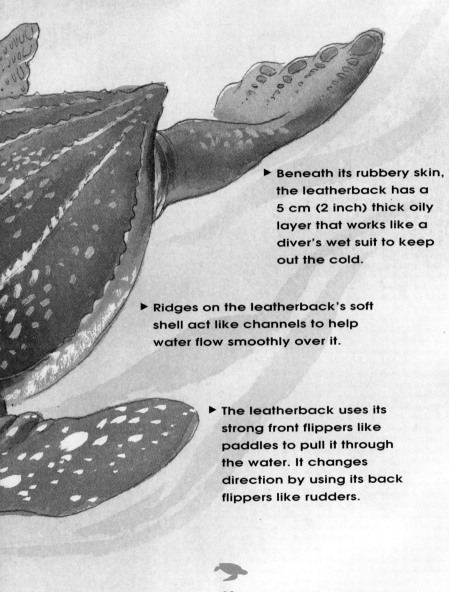

▶ Beneath its rubbery skin, the leatherback has a 5 cm (2 inch) thick oily layer that works like a diver's wet suit to keep out the cold.

▶ Ridges on the leatherback's soft shell act like channels to help water flow smoothly over it.

▶ The leatherback uses its strong front flippers like paddles to pull it through the water. It changes direction by using its back flippers like rudders.

The Jellyfish Eater

Leatherbacks eat all kinds of jellyfish — even poisonous ones such as Portuguese Man o'War. They will go anywhere in the ocean to feast on jellyfish — even into water too cold for other reptiles to survive. The leatherback's thick blubber and its special blood circulation helps it to stay warm even around icebergs.

Leatherbacks will also dive into very deep, dark waters to find jellyfish. Fortunately, many jellyfish glow like neon signs.

Where Do Leatherback Turtles Live?

Leatherback turtles live all around the world. Unlike other sea turtles that come close to land to find food, leatherbacks live and feed only in the open ocean.

Scientists know that leatherbacks spend the summer feeding in cold parts of the ocean, and also know that females return every two or three years to tropical beaches to lay their eggs. But nothing more is known about their travels.

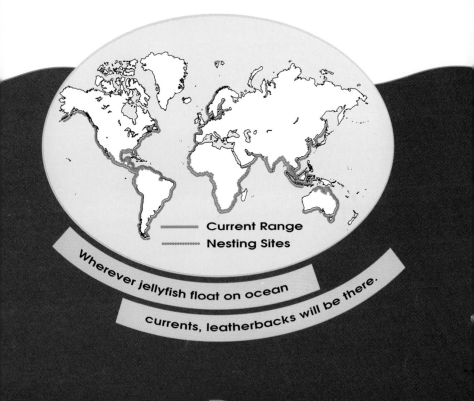

—— **Current Range**
········ **Nesting Sites**

Wherever jellyfish float on ocean currents, leatherbacks will be there.

Why Are Leatherback Turtles Endangered?

Leatherbacks all over the world are endangered. People have been collecting their eggs and killing females for their meat for many years. And as more buildings and marinas are built along tropical shores, the leatherbacks are losing many of their nesting beaches.

This leatherback was untangled from the net and returned safely to the sea.

Even leatherbacks at sea have not been safe. Many are killed and sold for food or oil, or they become tangled in fishing nets, where they drown. Others die from swallowing plastic bags that look almost exactly like jellyfish when they are filled with sea water.

What's Being Done?

People are helping leatherbacks in many parts of the world by switching off all lights near turtle beaches at nesting and hatching times. Why? Because lights often confuse leatherbacks so that they head towards them instead of the sea.

A protected turtle hatchery in Mexico. Half of all nesting leatherbacks nest on the west coast of Mexico.

Several Caribbean nations are working with the United Nations-sponsored Wider Caribbean Sea Turtle Recovery Team and Conservation Network (WIDECAST) to protect leatherbacks and their nesting beaches.

Ships are now forbidden by law to dump garbage into the ocean. Drift net fishing has been banned in some parts of the world. And fisherman are being encouraged to release any leatherbacks that they catch.

What Can You Do?

▶ Find out as much as possible about all endangered species and what is being done to help them. Then tell others what you have learned. Try these sources:

1. Your school and public libraries.

2. Canadian Wildlife Federation, 2740 Queensview Drive, Ottawa, ON K2B 1A2

3. Minister of Fisheries and Oceans, Centennial Towers, 15th Floor, 200 Kent Street, Ottawa, ON K1A 0E6 (for information on leatherbacks)

4. Sea Turtle Rescue Fund, Centre for Marine Conservation, 1725 DeSales Street N.W., Washington D.C., 20036

▶ Get involved in helping the environment. Take part in OWL and *Chickadee* Magazines' HOOT Club Awards Program. Write to OWL Magazine, 56 The Esplanade, Suite 306, Toronto, ON M5E 1A7.

Answers to Quiz

1-a, 2-c, 3-a, 4-c, 5-b and c, 6-a, 7-b